Meeting the Jet Man

David Knowles

TWO RAVENS
PRESS

Published by Two Ravens Press Ltd
Green Willow Croft
Rhiroy
Lochbroom
Ullapool
Ross-shire IV23 2SF

www.tworavenspress.com

The right of David Knowles to be identified as author of
this work has been asserted by him in accordance with the
Copyright, Designs and Patent Act, 1988.
© David Knowles, 2008.

ISBN: 978-1-906120-30-6

British Library Cataloguing in Publication Data. A CIP record
for this book can be obtained from the British Library.

Designed and typeset in Sabon by Two Ravens Press.
Cover design by David Knowles and Sharon Blackie.

Printed on Forest Stewardship Council-accredited paper by
Biddles Ltd., King's Lynn, Norfolk.

Mixed Sources
Product group from well-managed
forests, controlled sources and
recycled wood or fiber
www.fsc.org Cert no. TT-COC-002303
© 1996 Forest Stewardship Council
FSC

About the Author

In 1912 Bertrand Russell advised Wittgenstein to give up aviation in favour of philosophy. There was no similar advice forthcoming from the professors at Oxford when David Knowles abandoned his ambition to become an academic philosopher. He joined the RAF as a pilot in 1982. During the whole of his subsequent twenty-five-year RAF career David has been assigned to flying duties – they never managed to tie him to a desk job. For most of that time he has been on front-line Tornado ground-attack squadrons, amassing well over 3000 flight hours on one of the most potent airborne weapons systems of its day. From the closing years of the Cold War, through a decade of peace-keeping, the military victory in Iraq and then into its aftermath, David has been strapped into the cockpit trying to make sense of what he is seeing, experiencing and participating in. Awarded a Distinguished Flying Cross for actions during the opening phase of the invasion of Iraq, David has first-hand experience of aspects of modern warfare which have scarcely been touched upon in poetry before. He has recently retired from the RAF and founded Two Ravens Press publishing house with his wife and fellow writer Sharon Blackie.

Acknowledgements

All the Tornado crews I ever flew with have contributed in some way to this book, but particularly Andy Turk, the best man to have in your cockpit on a stormy night. My thanks to John Glenday for patiently steering me away from pitfalls and always taking my poems seriously enough to criticise them.

Introduction

My dreams about flying started some short time before my dreams about sex. With a similar whole-body sensation in the two cases. Shortly after that came an awareness of the great air battles of the Second World War – through feature films such as *The Battle of Britain* and *The Dambusters*. In my young mind some sort of fusion took place between these two threads – the flying and the warfare – which was in a sense quite arbitrary. There are many reasons to take to the air, warfare being only one of the more outlandish. The combination of themes was no less powerful for that – so powerful that it has taken me thirty years to glimpse the contingent nature of the connection. It is like finding that the smell you always associated with your mother's kitchen, and always took to be a function of her cooking, actually originated at the bakery next door.

I have just completed twenty-five years in the RAF. Those years were dedicated to the pursuit of excellence in flying and the application of my aircraft as a weapons system. Nothing more, nothing less. There can at times be an almost monastic completeness to the life of the fast-jet aircrew, the Jet Man.

Physically, flying is strange. The world is frequently upside down, your body often weighs four or five times its normal weight – or less than nothing. Great distances are consumed in seconds. Into that environment warfare intrudes. Or at least a tiny, upside-down frog's-eye glimpse of warfare intrudes. These poems are intended to take the reader into the cockpit and communicate that glimpse. For the strangeness of the sensations and the obscurity of some of the terminology I have no antidote but the poems themselves, plus a few explanatory notes at the back of the collection. Overcoming disorientation, both spatial and situational, is at the heart of military flying.

The sections of the collection are chronological – following the military operations in Iraq from the first Gulf War up to 2008, and my own involvement in them. However, the writing is not intended to be a 'working through', nor to provide a potted history, much less a resolution of moral issues. It is intended to bear witness to terrible events and what it is to actively participate in them. Why read such a book? Because it is easy for the natural distance between a society and its military to become a chasm of incomprehension. If this is allowed to happen, the decisions a society makes about the employment of military force are liable to be erroneous. I hope that these poems throw one thin thread across the chasm.

But before you go on operational duties, you first need to learn how to fly …

David Knowles
Lochbroom
2008

Contents

Part One
Never Enough
− 1991

TRICK OF THE TRADE	3
THROUGH THE SOUND BARRIER	4
VALLEY FLYING	5
FOLDING THE SHEETS	6
CLOSE FORMATION	8
INTO EXILE	10

Part Two
The Tightrope
1992-2002

MISSILE LAUNCH	13
AL KHARJ	15
FIRST BOMBS	16
MONSTROSITIES	18
SMART WEAPONS	22
WE WON'T BE BACK	23

Part Three
All Change
2003

OPENING NIGHT	27
POST MODERN WARFARE	29
MEETING THE JET MAN	30

FLAK   32
IT ISN'T A BLACKOUT   33
SO WHAT DOES IT *FEEL* LIKE?   35
THE SUNNI TRIANGLE   37
SPLIT THE SECOND – PUNCH THE CLOCK   39
A VICTORY OF SORTS   40
COMING HOME IN A SEAT   42
DINNER AT THE PETWOOD HOTEL   43

Part Four
The Bloody Garden Path
2004 –

BELIEVING THE INTELLIGENCE   47
AL UDEID   48
ONSHORE BREEZE   50
TIME TRAVEL IN MESOPOTAMIA   51
SNIPER IN BAGHDAD   52
THE ROAD TO NASIRIYAH   54
INCONCLUSIVE   56
THE GENERAL'S MORNING PRAYERS   58
STOP, REWIND, PLAY   60
THE LONG ARM OF THE LAW   62

Epilogue

DOWNWIND TO LAND FULLSTOP   65
DECOMMISSIONED   66

Notes

The feelings I don't have, I don't have.
The feelings I don't have, I won't say I have.

DH Lawrence

Part One

Never Enough
– 1991

TRICK OF THE TRADE

On an early solo with the Jet Man

Remember that first time?
We *had* to pull out
reflex-hard, stacking the Gs
like boxes of beans, just
to avoid smacking the ground.

We pulled right to the buffet
then gnawed on the bone of the lift curve –
good wings, giving all there was
and me, frozen with guilt
at throwing it all away.

But you, Jet Man, watched the tree-tops
like a card-player
counting the odds of impact.

I said 'Let's never do that again'
and you agreed, but the grin on our face
made me think you'd enjoyed it.

THROUGH THE SOUND BARRIER

No, there are no colours
we can still hear our thoughts
through air crammed so solid
nothing gets away.

Only goose-prickle shock
after shock-waves burst
through the skin of wings,
decorate the canopy with
hot thorns, the lambda feet
of brittle gas.

Still we push fuel through
a fat garden hose into burner cans,
bulldoze through these brambles
dragging at our sleeve
while the great salmon slab-tail
of this transonic Tornado grunts and holds
nose steady, scythe-line clear
through a forest of startled icicles,
leading shocks and trailing shocks clear-felled.
So mustn't we be quiet now
— out here ahead?

Alone, an old altimeter
round glass, much as it was,
curtseys in an LCD cockpit
to the passing of *Mach one*.

VALLEY FLYING

No Spitfire pirouette.
No delirious burning blue.
War-loaded gas-fat,
our jets foam at the mouth,
mud-wrestle with gravity –
call in favours to climb.

We ride the walrus,
press with both palms
on the sides of a narrow glen,
lever fatness through and belly
out of a hanging valley
onto the forest tops below.

FOLDING THE SHEETS

Nobody thinks it strange
if the high-altitude world
shrivels to a stillness;
the hours pass in slideshow,
carousel clicking while we blink.
Pass Lewis an unknown angry sea
there Iceland Nova Scotia Maine.
How would anything be strange
when it's fifty below
on the skin of this bubble;
we only barely inside
strapped tight in a warm hum,
nibbling biscuits between oxygen.

Fly lower, waking the nap of the earth –
now everyone has their notion of propriety.
How can you possibly *see* ...
– the lone climber on a snow-capped Ben –
is he waving? whether he is angry
or has failed almost to be angry
at our panel-beating of his landscape,
trading his peace for this spectacle
of steps cut into air?

Still lower, faster and faster
until abruptly the little gearbox seizes
the relevance of motion ceases
contingent as it was
on density altitude and entropy,
those dreams the night before,
the angle of the sun.

The wide field of view now all one place.
We hold the corners of the sheet and fold.

CLOSE FORMATION

We agreed on this dance of lead and follow
(I said 'I am his wingman,' or 'his wing' for short)
which put me here, six feet right,
looking in a mirror
at twenty tons of whispered screaming,
blowing a gusty wind
through the tree-tops of my canopy.
I could hop across the summer burn
that gurgles between his wingtip and mine.

We fly the simple exercise again
that flows with the formalities of tea
in a mid-power descent.
At four hundred knots, give or take
(this isn't an instrument approach;
it isn't in the numbers) we pull
up until the world loses sight,
the horizon closes its eyes and counts to ten,
the sky is a uniform brightness.

He must be rolling towards me –
his spoilers wave 'coo-ee',
the airspeed is bleeding…
have we stopped?

At the top of our manoeuvre
I balance an anvil over my head
by pushing on the bootlace that ties us.
No longer translating the language of eyes
into the dialect of a control column
(never *joystick*)
my arrow strikes the target with this dread:
just flying these bastard pit-bulls
is nowhere close to enough.

INTO EXILE

Lincolnshire, in a flying instructors' crewroom on the morning after Desert Storm commenced

We wake up burning
with their more vivid dream
etching through our lacquer
of ethos and pride
on down into the metal.

We breakfast-telly with the nation,
seated with zero-mission pilots,
below cheap manhood.
Too close to Stu and Jim and Graham
(now *combat-proven*)
to sidestep the shame.

I'll spare you tabloid metaphors
for warriors returning.
We swallow and gag
on the bitterness of them all,
as they step from the wings
of their opening night.

We are left with a taste in our mouths
which is not quite pineapple, nor panic, nor sadness.

Only that our ship has sailed.

Part Two

The Tightrope
1992-2002

MISSILE LAUNCH

Another hot fly-by day
minding our business up the Tigris
photographing the buzzing of flies.
F-16s riding shotgun –
unusual for the time of year.

Here on the Blue Deck
the upper balcony of the world
we skate, inverted
on the bottom of the sun-blind pool
on the top of the empty sky,
specks in a microscope slide.

Dreaming of a third dimension
we climb five thousand feet but nothing changes,
the white-cap mountains of Iran blink once
and resume their chain of thought.

Quietly – 'missile launch'

Then a long,
              matter-of-fact
                        Alabama guardsman pause.

Calmly – 'missile launch, left 8 o'clock.'

His pa flew in 'nam.
He knew how they would look.

2

You sweet nothings, passing ten thousand.
Mach three specks the size of telegraph poles,
the tiny drill bits at the left of the box,
burrowing into the sky.
No-one ever warned us you would be this beautiful,
wear your white satin gown to work.

So this is what speed looks like:
   first ten
   now fifteen
   now twenty thousand feet
   now above us
as fast and as slow as it took to mouth the words
leaving their statements sculpted in smoke
hooking over at thirty-five and detonating –
flourish and full stop at the end of a signature,
sound like soap-bubbles burst.

The horizon slides off a tilted table,
smashes into tiny pieces by the river.
We are no longer swimming
round the inside of a goldfish bowl.
We are four miles up
gripping anything solid.

AL KHARJ

We were truck-bombed out of Dhahran Airport. By god, there went the neighbourhood. Even generals get superstition when lightning strikes twice. Packed up the whole shooting match and set off into the desert. For a good deal longer than forty days and forty nights. In the absence of clouds we followed our flaming orders to Al Kharj, meaning, we understood, *as far away as you can get*. Chosen specifically for its crystal views of nothing, the safety of sand. It took a day for the nickname. We have a facility. "Al's Garage." Nobody invented it. He can have all the credit.

It took a week to unpack. A further week before we were certain. Then we just had to tell the general. 'Sir, we forgot two things – the journalists and the mission seem to have been left behind. Some sort of logistics cock-up with a crate of host nation sensibilities.' The general was pretty good about it, really. And eventually we found the missing journalists by the pool in Bahrain, though they weren't shifting.

Oh sure, they kept sweating us up to the top of any available hills. For a glimpse of the marshes draining away. The fall of Iraqi shot. The burning. We dutifully strained at the leash. But everyone at home knew full well that there was no diplomatic round in the chamber.

FIRST BOMBS

Haven't we reached the end of the tightrope? Sure
our first bombs have hit the target
silenced, for a time, this missile battery
and those voices
more dreaded than death over cocktails:

> '*Ah, flying – how wonderful…*
>> '*I always dreamt…*
>>> '*My eyesight of course…*
>> '*So have you…?*
> '*I mean, were you there in '91…?*
> '*No? No.*
>> '*Ah, but the flying, how wonderful…*'

I was so chuffed, you'd think it was Christmas
I said, after a suitable time had elapsed
(since impact and detonation),
'Mate, I could kiss your arse.'
which was not true, actually
as we were strapped into our respective cockpits
hundreds of miles from base.

2.

We hovered over the post-attack stills
like a couple with wedding photos
just back from the chemist.

Look, there's Rachel, the lavender suits her
and way over here the bits of the launcher
blown eighty yards!
Well, who'd have thought it?
And here are Chrissie and Len,
really *so* good of them
to come all that way.
See what's left of the control cabin?
Oh yes! Poor old Uncle Kevin –
he'll have had a thick head after that.

3.

Enter the intelligence officer:

'Whoa there, lads. We're terribly sorry
but the real missile site had left on a lorry.
All that you hit was a dummy transmitter
some pipes on a rail and the corporal's shitter.
And based on the photo-interpreter's call,
pretty sure the corporal wasn't there –
at all.'

Fuck. Are we really married?

MONSTROSITIES

We step out past the door-gunner's position. On the way here we flew past a refugee camp. I really wish that the UN-provided tarpaulins could have been a greener shade of blue. Like these peacocks on the landing zone. It would have been one of those really neat coincidences. But sadly, peacocks are – well – peacock-coloured. The UN tarpaulins are a sort of refuse-sack blue. Hundreds of bin bags with people in them, in a scrape of a hanging valley somewhere god-knows-where in relation to the peacocks at the landing zone. Somewhere, both the peacocks and the people, in Kurdish Iraq or Iraqi Kurdistan, depending.

The peacocks must be important. They live on a rocky knoll on the outskirts of the town we have come to visit. There is no vegetation. So they must be fed. So they must be important.

I don't know which town this is. What kind of a goddam pilot am I that I don't know which town this is – in my own back yard? I've been patrolling this area for the last six weeks. But not at low level. And the view from the back of a Blackhawk is none too sharp. There is a bit of a useless slit forwards, between the pilots, like looking out of a pillbox. And then there is a cut-up view through the side door, a rolling time-slice which is over before it is begun. Since I am only along for the ride, the hard-cases with the very big machine guns and bandoliers don't approve of the skinny Brit and I don't want to ask them where we are. Especially when the first thing I do when I'm out of the helicopter is pick up a peacock feather and look moronically at its colours in the sunshine. Breaks the spell of invincibility, you see. Which I think is maybe by-the-by when the other Blackhawk is still circling around pointing itself at things. You'd think they could afford one non-macho Brit.

The other Blackhawk eventually settles when the mayor shakes hands with the Colonel. I guess he's the mayor, though there is no chain of office. After that, our party splits. The medical team, around whom this whole performance is based, is escorted down to the main square. The man in the smart casuals with a combat jacket over the top is escorted to the mayor's house, along with the biggest of the big guys and a Sat-phone. I go with the medics. Which is just fine. The big guys now really don't like me anyway.

When I say medical team, I am being entirely accurate. One doctor, two fully trained paramedics plus bodyguards. Only they aren't here to do *direct* medical work. They are here to do *indirect* medical work. Which is to say, they are conducting a region-wide survey of how many doctors there are per thousand of population. In this town of, who knows, eight thousand people, there are no doctors. Which keeps the stats simple. There are, however, sick people. Specifically, sick children – who are quickly pushed through the crowd towards us once someone has translated the word 'medic'. This child has a mouth deformity that looks like someone put their clenched fist deep into the wet clay of its head and left a fist-void where the lips and mouth should be. This other has been badly burned. Some while ago. You know the smell. It won't be much longer now.

Yes, there is a lot of room in a Blackhawk. It's a big, grunty troop-carrier. No, our two are not full. No, it never crosses anyone's mind.

Our guards are told on the radio that the man with the smart casuals and the Sat-phone is doing rather better business than the *indirect* medics. We have an hour to kill.

This is a hill-town, built for safety in a bowl at the base of some serious snow-caps. The bowl has one exit, the road goes

19

steeply down onto the plain of northern Iraq. The buildings are pale and the sun shines so I am reminded of Assisi but with minarets. Occasionally I hear the peacocks. I wonder, do even the birds keep quiet at the evening call to prayer? We will be long gone by then.

There are roadside stalls selling the few things which are to be sold here. At this particular one I am forced to be astounded whether I wish to be or not. The man is selling money. From an open-fronted, flat-roofed shanty room half-built into the bank at the side of the road.

I say *selling* money because some of it he will let you have by the kilo, or at least in multiples of inches. He has old money issued with a face of a sprightly-looking Saddam Hussein on it – money long ago undercut by astronomical inflation. He has money issued by local governments and political organisations who once held sway in some area or another. And maybe they still do – if you care to take a punt on some of their money. Then there is money which he actually counts, but the value of which appears to shimmer in the heat. He has money of every colour and stacks of it. A seat at the side of his shop, in the shade, is made of a plank resting on bundles of used notes. Just in case this currency comes back into fashion, I suppose. He has many sorts of soft money. The idea of soft money tugs at a loose thread in my idea of everything. Money must have an exchange rate. Here it is bartered like a goat.

Since he has every sort of money besides dollars I go to offer him a five-dollar bill. Like when you offer a Scottish fiver to go on the foreign-currency notice-board in a bar. Nobody laughs. The shopkeeper spits and says something which nobody translates. The big guys would so hate me if they were here.

During the flight out of Iraq we pass by another refugee camp. Different valley but the same UN shelter-material. The sun catches it from another angle so that the colour is less vivid. But still it is nothing like peacock blue. There is something about the trip that has deeply disturbed me. I think through all I have seen. It's the thing about the money.

SMART WEAPONS

Bomb racks jut jagged
from the smooth-faired flush-fastened
belly of the jet.
No way to clothe their meaning.

There, just below the surface
swim the great green fish
hanging in the current
nosing across borders
pectoral fins sensing the wind.
Cyclopses' eyes never blink –
staring for guidance.

WE WON'T BE BACK

We always say it, every time:
'Well, we'll not be back here again.'
'Aye, thank heaven.'
Then take a photograph of the sign by the gate
ALI AL SALEM AIRBASE
or with the guard, beaming
with a dodgy rifle
and no real idea what we mean
but we might just be important.

Because it's over now
we can be a little sad to leave
the dugouts and hubble-bubble.

Since we won't be back.

Part Three

All Change
2003

OPENING NIGHT

The first night of the invasion of Iraq, 2003

Fate crowds out of a night sky
to press its face at the windows.
The crew-bus submerges,
trundles like a toy
two miles from Ops to aircraft
along a desert ocean floor.

The heavy water-column of duty
stacked above us
turns men, pairwise, into aircrews –
these twos; unidentical twins
spot-welded for the duration.

The driver – turned ferryman –
is paid in crumbs of history.
'What's the latest, drives?'
'Two-nil Chelsea; twenty to go.'
Coded smiles, old rivalries dropped
between officers and men.
So now he knows:
opening night.

We take our places for this short scene
playing passengers.
Desert dust on all-day sweaty collars
command and captaincy set down heavy
on an empty seat with helmets and torches
maps and ammunition.

Our loose formation
all nonchalance, nerves and improvised script.
'Hey, I know who killed Kennedy.
Tell you when I get back!'
On a mantelpiece in a long-gone mess
he leaves this half-drunk sherry glass
in close-up, double bluff.

Sinking into the silence of bit-parts
we fumble for phrases, clumsy rocks
lifted from the bottom of the stream
levering on a future already laid out
on the cold slab of hindsight.

We surface suddenly grateful
at the arc-lit fins
of warplanes tended by armourers.
As welcome as curtain-up,
the promise of a full house.

.

POST MODERN WARFARE

Ragi Omar flinches twice
at the tell-tale double-tap
of a warhead I took to Disneyland
four hours ago, recorded live.
Fast reactions, that lad.

Tinkerbell gunners still spray the sky
with out-of-range magic dust
that falls rattling in the streets.

Fifty minutes later than hours earlier,
landed grateful at an *undisclosed desert location*
we sit in the cab of a fire-truck
in the pitch at the end of the strip
lights-out unscheduled Brits
a clatter of bits 'coming in hung!'
gate-crashing their southern-flank war
scrounging a tank of gas.

The fire-chief (from Montana originally –
'God's country,' so he tells me)
is talking four-to-the-dozen.
'Those poor bastards won't know what's hit 'em.'
Shock and Awesome, live on CNN.
I really should have seen it.

MEETING THE JET MAN

Been chasing the Jet Man, on the tail of this piece for twenty years. Through crewrooms and airshows and bars. Always unavailable for interview, always declining to comment. Through training, through exercises, through deployments – at most a grin. Living behind the visor. Guessed at. Implied. Secretive and secret. I got close once or twice – blagged through security. He'd skipped out the back door. All I found were some junior aircrew reading The Telegraph. Chatty, but unsure of themselves.

Tonight of all nights there is some sort of foul-up. The sky over Kuwait bleeds quietly through a slit in the moon and there are 3 minutes and 45 seconds before crew-in. Even after banter with the groundcrew, the weapon checks, stringing it out: *Re-check that fuze-arming lanyard, would you, Chief?* The Jet Man is available. Not his face. But a face is not really required. His shadow, then. On a concrete blast-wall the size of a movie screen. *Like a drive-in for warplanes. Techies better get their skates on!* Funny guy, the Jet Man.

How does he feel about the moon, this sliver of desert portent, this cool light soothing the burning sand?

He thinks about 40 millilux. Enough light to see another aircraft's skin. Through the tubes. Enough to fly close aboard without lights. Comfortable. *There is great beauty…* Only with fewer syllables. Speech clipped. Sheared away by superhets over the years like a No. 2 crew-cut.

Drowned out by overflight of returning rotaries, he becomes radio-silent. A full-body hand-puppet in the beam of the moon-projector. G-suit, swagger pants, fat-belly survival vest, feet apart like John Wayne. Enough kit to sink a fish out of water in foil packs. Morphine and a spare clip for the worst. One hand plays a rabbit, the other a bulge you'd swear was a sidearm from a cowboy costume, and another hangs by his side.

We look at our luminous watch, perfectly synchronised. Time's up.

FLAK

Flak spits grit in a clear sky.
Contrary: black on a clear day
white in a storm.
Not announcing itself – well,
maybe some fairy lights on the ground –
but who knows at this height.
Some events are simply not
connected to anything at all.

So, flak
not getting to where it has arrived
there
just
more sudden than itself.

IT ISN'T A BLACKOUT

It isn't a blackout.
They just haven't fixed the lights.
Hit your shins twice
as you turn left out of Ops,
fluorescent-blind; next time you'll remember.

The night-shift is pausing for breath,
hunched shoulders and a fag.
Pacing themselves up the steep, dark hours.
No thanks mate – haven't smoked in years.

The tide of the war is a long way out now
and you can't hear the waves –
not from here any more.
We just fly north-west until somebody needs us,
unload, then hurry home.
Could have had another hour in bed –
but we tend not to.

That red ash in the corner
the bulky-black absence
of glow from the concrete –
my nav and his intercom voice
silent amongst the murmurs
of professional military moans.

He has no use for my fears:
that isn't how we work.
But 3AM is a miserable time to launch
when sun-up will come
with a sticky mouth and pissing in a bag.

Good to stand next to him in the dark
and not to say a word.

SO WHAT DOES IT *FEEL* LIKE?

There is this smooth ridge
on the front face of the throttles
like the big sinew on the back
of an old man's hand.
My fingers rest there.

There is the smell of hardly anything
mixed with hot wiring
and the silent hum of avionics
deep in the loft of the fuselage.
Over all a watercolour wash of AVTUR.

There is a noise comes into our silence
close to the place we are going.
The sound of *them and us* –
men fighting –
an intrusion of lock-on and jamming
a rag-bag of coordinates and talk-ons
heavy static, numbing interference.

There is a chink in the curtains
sometimes a flicker in the breeze
where doubt gets into a night cockpit
while my back is turned.

There is the familiar surprise
as I wait four long, drawn-out milliseconds
thumb hard down on the pickle button
held to account
for not following the checklist
for the failure of the mission
for the wrong side's casualties
the humiliation ...
ended by the *knock-knock* of release.

There is a trip home, racks empty.
A hop, skip and a jump in an old jet
suddenly a young girl dancing
foot-light around finals.

Nothing can touch us now.

THE SUNNI TRIANGLE

These are not the names of warriors
who have displeased the gods
scrawled on a scrap of notepad
feint and margin, block capitals
in damn-it hurry-up blue biro
then hand-carried to my cockpit
one engine running
sweating with the lid up
jumpy about the fuel temperatures
drumming four fret fingers on the side-rail.

These are only so simply the targets
to this many decimals north,
to this many decimals east.
In the spell of a satellite constellation
we are all one world now.
Neither here nor there.

2.

We jitter down the target run
in and out of sight, of cloud, of certainty
and a supposed division on the move.
Expecting El Alamein, seeing suburbia.

The paper tiger of Medina
hasn't folded yet. We take their silence
for ambush, they take our overflight
as the will of God.

3.

The bombs at last release us
to fall upwards away,
barrelling into cloud where we never see the splash.
Maybe that's why those bombs still fall,
lost in the Sunni triangle,
stubborn as Gulf Stream eels.
Maybe now those three just detonated
and cast-iron shrapnel, sharper than glass,
light as an axe-head on the down-stroke,
has split the carrier bag of a soldier's guts
and I'm finally spilling the beans.

SPLIT THE SECOND – PUNCH THE CLOCK

No more ground to cover.
No take-a-deep-breath.
This decision is screaming *'Now!'*
and *Now* has no depth
just a line on hindsight's tab
the hot stink of a straight-finger jab.

Release the weapon.

Punch the slow swiss coaming-mounted stopwatch
ease up and right and throttled-back wait
for the second-hand thin as an eggshell crack
to fall like a mallet on the first second
of forty seconds to impact.

A VICTORY OF SORTS

Up-country in a blur
so dark it must be night.
My inner ear will not be told
the wings are level, the nose
is not vertical, these lights in the desert
are not stars.

Clocks in GMT say nothing of the sun,
tick-tock the war's private time.
Maps rock underfoot, see-saws in midstream
washed out by the speed of advance.

Only this great white belly
floats fixed in the sky –
the moon-bladder of fuel, so fat
you could prick it with a pin.
Refuellers pushed beyond now
where they shot at us last week.

Is this victory? 'Aye, but many's
the slip 'twixt probe and drogue'
cracks the angry blue spark at 'contact!'
– lightning as long as your thumb.

For now fuel flows.
That is enough on a stormy night.

2.

Fumbling for targets on the stairs
between floors of a nightclub
lights-off bass-line oozing through walls
chatter on three frequencies
unknown faces crowd out of the darkness
and into darkness grope
for bannisters and coordinates.
Fresh crowds peer at sweaty homebounds
recognising nobody.
The air armada crosses itself in the dark.

Only ... once there was Jock,
disembodied on Tanker Primary,
a familiar voice digging us in the ribs:
'Ahoy, losers – hit anything yet?'

COMING HOME IN A SEAT

Our not dying is final.

Stamped "collectively alive"
we are returned to sender, unused.
Except for Kevin and a quiet Welsh nav
soup-tureened, smithereened
by a Patriot's ten-k warhead.

> *The crack of the outgoing launch,*
> *that supersonic jack-in-the-box*
> *as I nodded off, post-mission*
> *struck through with last words 'what the …?'*
> *before a long sleep.*

But these were friendly deaths
with no best side for the camera
denied their varnish
of enemy fire.

Us they send home in a seat,
parcel-post on a plane, not met
by bands of black
or weeping.
We are not carried off the ramp
nor punctuated with a bullet.

DINNER AT THE PETWOOD HOTEL

617 Dambuster Sqn's Wartime Mess

Papery old men, barely enough weight to stay on the ground.
Held down by age-spotted sweethearts lest they fly again.
The gong sounds them in to dinner, then as now,
stiffens them into a cliché of their own invention
muttering incantations to '*Fallen Comrades!*'

Seated together they rise like bubbles
through the deep water of their life.
The ramblings of age fall clean away
clipped back by intercom's topiary of meaning
blown skyward in the gale howling
down a fuselage shot to hell.

Their wives stare down at dessert,
bear the brunt again of their finest hours.

Part Four

The Bloody Garden Path
2004 –

BELIEVING THE INTELLIGENCE

Is this fucking Disneyland or what?

It's another palace, mate.

I'm tired of this fucker's palaces. How many palaces did he need?

This is the Baghdad Airport Palace. There's tunnels to the terminal.

It's a mile bloody square. It's a mile-bloody-square lake with twirly islands.

Guess he needed a bigger moat!

Oh aye, and there's frigging Jaws, or dolphins or something. We get any lower? I'm sure that's dolphins. In the fucking desert.

Looks like dolphins to me. Never mind WMD. The fucker had dolphins in the desert.

Bastard.

AL UDEID

The roots of our new desert airbase
push deep in the soil of ambition.
Fertilised by thin-crust hatred,
constantly hydrated
in sprinkles of jet noise.

The runway is a giant's footprint
stamped by the sweaty Gulf
visible from space
while we ants crawl
from breakfast to sortie brief;
aircrews flattened into shadows
by the weight of the sun.

We pass by these others
born to the heat from Karachi or Peshawar
happy by birth-right
chattering like sparrows silenced
by our presence.
They shrink back
into overalls and head-scarves.
Only the eyes remain to note
our hats and insignia, the beads of sweat
so soon after sun-up.

They concrete and weld
the fortress of a super-power –
'Third Country Nationals'
watched over by bored guards
fresh-faced from Milwaukee or Arkansas –
send home good money and dreams.

I forget myself with a smile.
He nods.
Worlds kiss, blink,
resume their orbits.

We'll make up for it later.

ONSHORE BREEZE

Sea-hot air drip-wets the darkness
steps out of the shower
to pad barefoot over Doha.

Hard into the soles of its feet
this city's rough aspirations,
baked in the shadows
of Manama and Dubai.
Should have worn sandals.

No matter –
the knees-up wincing ballet
of children on a rocky beach
sees it safe inland
settled cross-legged on a dune.

The desert expects his distant cousin.
Puts a towel down ready
to save the upholstery.
Soaks up the wet backside of the Gulf.

TIME TRAVEL IN MESOPOTAMIA

There's time-travel in Mesopotamia. The electricians are on to it – but the wiring is a mess. It only makes sense when you drop your mask:

Al just bombed Habaniyah – narrowly missing his father, who was stationed there in the '50s.

The Ziggerat of Ur is still pissed off that Alexander rode right past. But that old Soviet triple-A, always banging away at us to no effect, would have spooked his horse.

Al Qaeda just failed to drop the bridge that a pair of F-16s hit ten years ago – only the bombs dudded and then the show was over.

And sure as shit that's Gavin Maxwell, looking for giant otters in the desert. Hang on fella, someone has put the plug back in. Water's on the way.

'Mate, you OK? Put your mask back on.'

SNIPER IN BAGHDAD

In-flight re-tasking in support of a US army patrol in Baghdad

Out of the blue air:
'Scandal Flight, contact Dogwood 41 for tasking.'

Roger that, Scandals en route.

> *There's a needle in my haystack*
> *and my buddy's lost his mind*
> *if you could guide a bomb down here*
> *that would be very kind*

Copied, Dogwood 41, what's your status?

> *Static … awaiting casevac.*
> *(Lots more static).*

Can AWACS see him?
My arse!
Can the satellites see him?
Not bloody likely!
Can I fucking see him?

I'm looking at an A to Z
the scale is 1 to 1
if I could only eyeball him
I'd shoot him with my gun

Only there's no street names up here
Ten minutes to get eyes on my soldier –
let alone the enemy.

Dogwood 41 going mobile, southbound RTB.

Scandals re-re-tasked in the north.

Have a good one.

See you later.

Crazy Brits!

THE ROAD TO NASIRIYAH

1992

Fly with us for the first time, eyes sliding
from horizon to horizon on the smooth ice
of the open desert. We'll hammer in some fixpoints.
You grab the handrail of a single hardcore track
northbound to Nasariyah.

But how easily the sand throws off
the tattered string vest we impose –
those latitudes and longitudes.

The Bedou find our coordinates unattended,
carry them off in a pick-up.

2001

Fly with us up the road to Nasiriyah.
Familiar at fifty miles out
the sagging curve of the four-lane bypass
cups its gentle hand
around the sacred invisible city
cloaked in its dust.

Overhead now
you wonder at those dark scars fading?
"Craters on the moon
with splash of black flour."
Only a catalogue entry
in some squadron's history.

2003

Tonight we have company
on the road to Nasiriyah
which no longer goes to town
but terminates at the Main Supply Route.
All change, all change!

We've short-circuited the country –
one spark from Mosul to Basrah.

2006

Don't bother flying with us
not up this road again
the road to Nasiriyah
this bloody garden path.

INCONCLUSIVE

Way out west in the desert. The four-colour map theorem breaks down. Jordan, Syria, Saudi, Iraq – they all flow into each other. Maps agree to disagree. Crazy things happen. Lawrence of Arabia still northbound to Damascus. Who knows? Sand keeps covering his tracks. Water comes out of rock, goes nowhere, makes a single orange tree grow. Running firefights between shadowy forces who weren't there yesterday and won't be there next week. This is not Baghdad.

It took a whole lot to get us here. Right here. Right now. Surveillance, comms, command – the greatest *camera obscura* the world has ever seen. A general in the southern gulf peering intently at an acre of desert in western Iraq. One jet, one Toyota pick-up truck, a *bongo*, a *technical*. Hell for leather. The border is close and the tide is in right now. But not close enough. Suspension must be shot to hell. Mind, smooth enough up here. A mile up the way. Looks like he's in a hovercraft on a sea of dust. We have clearance. Stand-off. Ramp down, unthreatened. Humming.

At a hundred feet there are suddenly two of us. The shadow and me. Tight. Two spiny black beetles rolling our ball of sound over the desert. Not any old sound. Solid sound. Punch-you-hard-in-the-guts sound. The Toyota does a funny little squiggle like people do signing a cheque. Is stationary. We arc up and left. I always like to go left. It is a weakness. Back overhead, more slowly, made our point. They are out of the truck, kneeling in the sand. We confirm the heading with a ring-laser inertial. Not a bad guess at all.

I take us back to the perch, just for good form's sake. They wait. Not knowing we are unarmed. Butt-naked. Diplomatic restrictions, you see. Temporary glitch in the system. Anyhow, we are out of gas and eastbound. The general has something interesting on the go near Kirkuk.

THE GENERAL'S MORNING PRAYERS

The General's name is George.
He looks like your uncle, his smile
is better than pocket money.

The General sits without ceremony
he gets the big picture
through six senses, digested quickly,
assimilated immediately, known already.
Two wars, one airborne armada.
His call.

You met George once on a fishing trip
he gave you his killer fly –
just in case you were finding it tough.
Which you were.
He'd had 'one or two'.
Yeah, right: and the rest.

A voice without a flicker tells him:
'Yesterday there were eight ...'
'The Paddington train is late ...'
'Coalition Force members killed in action ...'
'Buffet service will be available ...'

George and the General pause for effect.

Twenty colonels' pens hover.
A hundred captains stop the press.
A thousand aircrew take a breath.

'Let's send these folk on their way.'
(To hell, we surmise – 'They sure as shit
ain't goin' to Montana.')

The General's voice echoes down
the chain of command
where the distant-most echo
flattens a mountain.

STOP, REWIND, PLAY

Debrief with cockpit video

STOP

Nothing left to bury
not in this frame.
We cannot count the dead
in the sticky black soot
that settles on washing lines
and ink-pads the streets
so they record the vehicle signatures
for the rebuttal stills
that will be taken an hour later
that now lie on the intelligence desk.

Instead we'll tally the living and subtract.
Give that to the military;
at least we keep accounts.

REWIND

*Watch the left of the screen from fifteen seconds time to
impact.*

PLAY

We tug on puppet strings again
Our *'Encore!'* sets the dead men dancing
almost late for *'places, please!'*
but bent to the inevitable.

Not at all sure of the script
they may still turn quickly back
kneel, and cover-fire
while the last grains of sand
surge from a waisted past
free of a cluttered future.

The clearance to drop stated fifteen.
Combatants in contact.
We count twelve.
Close enough.

STOP

No ... wait.
What is *he* doing, low central,
at three seconds to impact ?
What? Can they hear it coming?
He kneels
not firing
hands clasped over his balls.

THE LONG ARM OF THE LAW

Reaching round the world
the hugging arms of B-1 overnight
in do-the-business class
refuelled by prior appointment
the black bear laden
with a black-snow storm.
'Son, it's a big deal
to empty a whole B-1.'

Heard a general say that once.
Not a general prone to exaggeration.

Epilogue

DOWNWIND TO LAND FULLSTOP

From the manual of radio telephony: fullstop landing
– a landing with no subsequent take-off (now obsolete;
absorbed into the meaning of landing)

'Tower, Snake 2 is downwind to land ... fullstop.'

We land a crosswind kiss, last touch
of rudder puts the nose straight
the record straight between air and earth
before we roll to the end
stop-drilling cracks in the voices
that chant the final checklist.

Not now, not here in the cockpit –
no loose articles of emotion, just:
    'Pitot heaters ...?'
    'Pitot and windscreen heaters off ...'

DECOMMISSIONED

1.

What'll we do now, you and I,
together through all these years?
My angel movie skin with wings
with tickets to the sky.

What'll we do now, uniform,
now that we are forbidden?

Will we remember the time we paraded,
the confetti and champagne?
Should we leave it at black armbands?
Could we meet just once a year
in private, reminisce …

No?
Out of the question.
I agree.

2.

Some years later, when the Squadron is about to move to a new airfield, they find a uniform. It hangs behind some boxes in the back of a locker at the far end of the hangar. It has no distinguishing marks, has been stripped of its honours. No fingerprints except for a patch less faded where wings would have been. They imagine it belongs to the Jet Man. There is no forwarding address.

Notes

Trick of the Trade. 'Gs' or G-forces are the result of an aircraft, or any other vehicle, turning a corner – in this case pulling out of a steep dive towards the ground.

Through the Sound Barrier. As an aircraft accelerates towards the speed of sound, entering the transonic regime of flight, shock waves start to form which appear, to an infra-red camera, like thorns or spikes bursting out of the aircraft. The thickening of the shock wave at the aircraft's skin is called a 'lambda foot'. The pattern changes until eventually a speed is reached when the individual shock waves are left behind.

As the aircraft finally breaks free of the shock-waves the needle of a traditional altimeter will briefly dip a few hundred feet then recover.

Close Formation. The flight manoeuvre described is known as a 'wingover' – a steep climb is followed by the application of bank up to or exceeding ninety degrees, allowing the aircraft to descend and regain airspeed. In a Tornado the aircraft is banked by a combination of taileron deflection and lift 'spoilers' on the wings. As the lead aircraft of the formation rolls towards his wingman the opening and closing of the spoilers are clearly visible.

Al Kharj. During the First Gulf War an American accommodation block at Dhahran was destroyed by an extremely improbable direct hit by a Scud missile. In 1996 a truck bomb destroyed another accommodation block at the same airfield. Soon afterwards the coalition presence at Dhahran was moved to Al Kharj in the heart of the Saudi desert.

Post Modern Warfare. 'Hung ordnance' is the term used to describe bombs or missiles on an aircraft which have malfunctioned in some way – remaining on the aircraft after the crew have attempted to release them.

So What Does it Feel *Like?* 'AVTUR' is aviation turbine fuel, a high flash-point type of kerosene with an almost sweet smell.

'Pickle button' is the slang name for a bomb-release button.

'Finals' is the name for the portion of flight just prior to landing. In a military jet this will often be flown as a descending one hundred and eighty-degree turn.

The Sunni Triangle. The Medina Division was an Iraqi Republican Guard armoured formation fielded on the southern approaches to Baghdad during the invasion.

A Victory of Sorts. 'Probe and drogue' is an air-to-air refuelling system which requires the pilot to fly his or her aircraft such that a probe on the receiving aircraft fits into a trailing basket (drogue) on the refueller. At night a static discharge is often visible as the probe and drogue make contact.

'Tanker Primary' refers to the radio frequency on which air-to-air refuelling operations are co-ordinated.

Coming Home in a Seat. During the 2003 invasion of Iraq an RAF Tornado was shot down by an American Patriot missile as the crew were returning to Ali al Salem airbase. The missile was launched near to where I was sleeping. The Patriot makes a characteristic, supersonic 'crack' as it leaves the ground.

Time Travel in Mesopotamia. The airfield at Habaniyah, just west of Baghdad, was an RAF base in the '50s and a target for RAF bombing in Desert Storm.

The abbreviation of anti-aircraft artillery is spoken as 'triple-A'.

Gavin Maxwell lived with the Marsh arabs of south-eastern Iraq for a time, studying, amongst other things, a species of giant otter. After the First Gulf War Saddam Hussein systematically drained the marshes with a view to eradicating Shia Muslim resistance. As well as a human tragedy this was an ecological disaster. The task of re-flooding the marshlands was started soon after the end of the 2003 invasion.

Sniper in Baghdad. 'AWACS' stands for Airborne Warning and Control System. It is an airliner modified for surveillance and for command and control functions.

'Casevac' is short for Casualty Evacuation.

The Road to Nasiriyah. 'Main Supply Route'. An advancing force will establish one or more main supply routes for logistics and re-enforcement. In the 2003 invasion the motorway joining Kuwait to Baghdad was given this function. For much of its length it lies to the south of the Euphrates, passing around the sacred city of An Nasariyah in a sweeping curve almost like a cupped hand.

STOP, REWIND, PLAY. 'Rebuttal stills'. Film from the cockpit and still images from reconnaissance sensors are gathered before, during and after an air attack for a number of purposes. One purpose is 'rebuttal' – whereby false claims of collateral damage can be refuted by photographic evidence of the attack.

The Long Arm of the Law. The B-1 is a US heavy bomber with enormous payload and global reach. They are painted a uniform black.

Poetry from Two Ravens Press

Castings: by Mandy Haggith
£8.99. ISBN 978-1-906120-01-6. Published February 2007

Leaving the Nest: by Dorothy Baird
£8.99. ISBN 978-1-906120-06-1. Published July 2007

The Zig Zag Woman: by Maggie Sawkins
£8.99. ISBN 978-1-906120-08-5. Published September 2007

In a Room Darkened: by Kevin Williamson
£8.99. ISBN 978-1-906120-07-8. Published October 2007

Running with a Snow Leopard: by Pamela Beasant
£8.99. ISBN 978-1-906120-14-6. Published January 2008

In the Hanging Valley: by Yvonne Gray
£8.99. ISBN 978-1-906120-19-1. Published March 2008

The Atlantic Forest: by George Gunn
£8.99. ISBN 978-1-906120-26-9. Published April 2008

Butterfly Bones: by Larry Butler
£8.99. ISBN 978-1-906120-24-5. Published May 2008

For more information on these and other titles, and for
extracts, reviews and author interviews, see our website.

**Titles are available direct from the publisher, post & packing-
free (in the UK, and for a small fixed fee overseas) at**
www.tworavenspress.com
Visit our online magazine, CORVACEOUS, and read our daily
blog about life as a small publisher on a remote north-west
Highland croft.